True or False?
Tests Stink!

by Trevor Romain
& Elizabeth Verdick

free spirit
Works for kids®
PUBLiSHiNG®

Library of Congress Cataloging-in-Publication Data

Romain, Trevor.
    True or false? Tests stink! / by Trevor Romain and Elizabeth Verdick.
        p.   cm.
    Summary: Offers proven strategies, practical advice, and information to help readers survive in all kinds of test situations, including tips on overcoming test anxiety and procrastination, preparing for tests, the pros and cons of guessing, and more.
    ISBN 1-57542-073-2 (pbk.)
    1. Test-taking skills Juvenile literature. 2. Test anxiety Juvenile literature. [1. Test-taking skills.] I. Verdick, Elizabeth. II. Title.
    LB3060.57 .R66 1999
    372.126—dc21

                                                                99-37462
                                                                    CIP
                                                                     AC

10 9 8 7 6 5 4 3 2 1

Free Spirit Publishing Inc.
400 First Avenue North, Suite 616
Minneapolis, Minnesota 55401-1724
(612) 338-2068
help4kids@freespirit.com
www.freespirit.com

Dedication

For my brother Steve and my sister Elise,
who both get A's in the "terrific people test."
                    —Trevor

For Mr. Glasser, an art teacher who believed
in me, and for Mrs. Alexander, an English
teacher who taught me a love for writing.
These two teachers showed me that school
can be cool.
                    —Elizabeth

Contents

Introduction

Do Tests + You = **PANIC?** You're not the only one. Students of all ages get nervous at test time.

Tests are tough. Tests are a pain. Tests can be hard to take.

Sad but true, you have to take tests all the way through school. Spelling tests, math tests, chapter tests, unit tests, standardized tests . . . the list goes on and on.

If you were to line up all these tests end to end, you could probably cover the top of the Great Wall of China! (If you don't know what the Great Wall of China is, look it up. Someday, you might be tested on it.)

Here's the good news: You can become a better test taker. You can feel more confident (and less stressed) before, during, and after tests. This book tells you how.

Tests? Blech!

Do you think tests are pests? Like a fly buzzing in your ear and landing in your lunch? Too bad there's no such thing as "Test Repellent." Just a spray would keep tests away.

P.S. You could grow up to be the brilliant inventor of this spray—but that would mean doing well on your science tests!

Why do students all over the world have to take tests? Is it some kind of punishment? (Nope.) Is it the grown-ups' way of making kids' lives miserable? (Not really.) Then . . .

Because tests *test* you (which is why they're called tests, of course). They make you memorize those facts, numbers, names, words, and dates you've been learning about in school.

Think of tests not as pests, but as a way to learn and grow and **SHOW WHAT YOU KNOW.**

7

Some tests are *really* hard, like standardized or proficiency tests (some of them go on for days!). You sit there like a robot neatly filling in rows of little circles until someone announces **"STOP! PUT YOUR PENCILS DOWN!"** (causing you to drop your pencil like a hot potato).

You'd probably rather eat worms than take one of these tests.

Or sniff rotten eggs . . .

Or even kiss a snapping turtle.

Like it or not, tests are here to stay. No, dialing 911 won't help!

Is this an EMERGENCY?

What will? Learning to do your best on tests. The trick is knowing two things about every test:

1. what's on it (as much as possible)

2. how to take it (keep reading for tips).

Test SOS

SOS is a code for getting help. You can think of learning to be a better test taker as breaking a secret code!

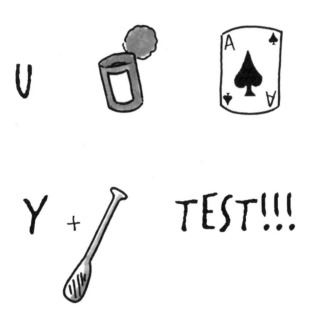

Test-Taking Hints

#1: Be test wise. Pay special attention whenever your teacher says something like "This will be on the test." Put a star next to this information in your notebook.

#2: Be a test detective. Watch and listen for other clues your teacher may give about what's going to be on the test. For example, if your teacher underlines certain facts on the blackboard or says "You need to know this," take the hint!

#3: Take a practice test. Ask your teacher if you can take a practice test to sharpen your skills for the real test. (An *extra* test means *extra* help.) Check your answers and see which topics you need to study more.

#4: Make a test-survival kit. Before the test, get your kit ready. Pack lots of pens or pencils (sharpen them first and make sure they have good erasers), notes you want to look at, a calculator (if you're allowed to bring one), and anything else that might help you.

#5: Dress for success. Wear comfortable clothes and shoes. You may even want to dress in layers (wear a T-shirt under a sweater, for example) so you can take something off (or put something on) if you're too hot or cold.

Top-Secret Stuff!

Here are a few things your teachers probably never told you about tests.

- When you don't know an answer, it's okay to guess—unless you get points taken away for wrong answers.

- On true-or-false tests, look for words like *sometimes, most,* and *rarely.* Often, answers containing these words are **TRUE.** Answers that contain words like *always* or *never* are usually **FALSE.**

- On multiple choice or matching questions, use *the process of elimination.* This means crossing off the choices you know aren't correct. This helps bring you closer to the right answer.

- Your first answer is usually correct, so don't go back and change it unless you took a wild guess.

- You can look for answers or hints in other questions on the test!

During a test, do you feel as stiff as a board? This means you're tense. Or maybe you have the opposite problem: You turn into a spaghetti noodle and slump over your desk. **WAKE UP!** You have a test to take.

Good Test Posture

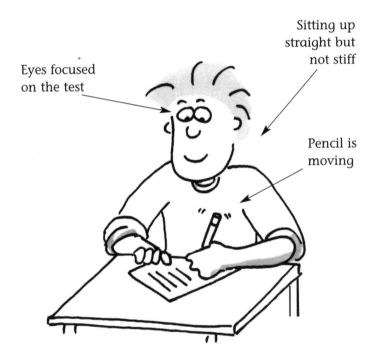

Eyes focused on the test

Sitting up straight but not stiff

Pencil is moving

Terrible Test Posture

Pencil balanced on upper lip

Leaning way back to get the best view of the clock ⟶

Feet in aisles, ready to trip someone

Tip: Practicing good test posture helps you stay sharp.

Have you ever sat near one of the world's most annoying test takers?

The Pencil Roller

The Scribbler

The Heavy Sigher

The Hiccuper

The Cougher

The Fidgeter

The Mumbler

The Endless Pencil Sharpener

Don't let these students distract you! If you can't concentrate, ask your teacher (quietly) if you can move to an empty seat at the back of the room. If you have a learning difficulty, it may help to take tests in a separate room where you won't be disturbed. Ask your teacher or principal if this is an option for you (*before* your next test).

Pop Quiz #1

Answer True or False.

The night before a test, it's a good idea to:

1. Think positive thoughts like
   "I'm ready for this."   T   F

2. Look over your notes in a quiet place.   T   F

3. Review information that still isn't clear.   T   F

4. Call a friend for help, if you need it.   T   F

5. Ask your mom or dad to quiz you.   T   F

6. Review your practice test, if you took one.   T   F

7. Get a good night's sleep.   T   F

Answers: You're a Quiz Whiz if you know they're all true. Give yourself an A+ and remember that pop quizzes (PQs) don't have to mean Pretty Queasy.

Bonus Question

Multiple Choice.

The morning before a test, it's best to eat:

A. chocolate-covered doughnuts with sprinkles

B. yogurt or toast, with some fruit

C. bacon and eggs, pancakes (heavy on the syrup and butter), a few sausage links, and hashbrowns

D. nothing but soda with caffeine

Answer: B. Experts say kids who eat a healthy breakfast do better in school. You can get off to a smart start by eating a *nutritious* breakfast that fills you up without weighing you down. Avoid too much sugar and caffeine, which give you a short burst of energy and then leave you worn out, or greasy foods, which can make you feel tired. Never take a test on an empty stomach—it's hard to think when you're hungry, and your stomach might make weird noises during the test!

Tips for Test Day

#1: Arrive early. Give yourself extra time to review your notes and get ready.

#2: Read or listen to the directions. You may want to start answering test questions right away,

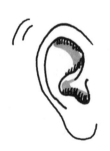

but make sure you understand the directions first. Look over the whole test so you know what to expect.

#3: If you have a question, ask! If the directions are unclear or a test question doesn't make sense, don't wait to ask the teacher for help.

#4: Check over your answers. Before you hand in your test, make sure you responded to every question. Are you satisfied with your answers? If not, go back to any questions that you had trouble with and think about your answers.

Pop Quiz #2

Multiple Choice.

If other students finish their test before you do, you should:

A. assume they're all smarter than you

B. ignore them and focus on your own test

C. rush to catch up

D. give up, fold your test into a paper airplane, and shoot it out the nearest window

Answer: B. Don't worry, hurry, or give up. *Faster* doesn't always mean *smarter*. There's no reward for being the first to finish. Take the time you need.

P.S. Did you know some studies have shown that answer "B" is the right one 40 percent of the time? Remember this in case you have to make a guess!

Test-Taking Do's and Don'ts

When your teacher announces the test:

DO ask what kind of test it will be and what it will cover.

DON'T become test obsessed! As in . . .

Or two seconds after the test ends . . .

When you don't know the answer to a test question:

DO move on to the next question and come back to the other one later. You don't have to answer the test questions in the exact order they appear.

DON'T answer the question by writing everything you know *except* the answer to the question. You may hope your teacher will be impressed with all your knowledge, but she doesn't need X-ray vision to see right through you!

AND NEVER cheat. Even if you take just one tiny peek at your neighbor's test, you're cheating, and cheating is against school rules. Besides, you may get the right answer but not because you've learned it or earned it.

If someone tries to cheat off your test:

DO cover up your test and continue. Later, you can tell your teacher what happened.

DON'T leap up from your desk and scream "Hey everybody! This cheater is cheating off me!!" while pointing at the guilty person. This will make it very difficult for the other students to continue with the test.

Test Stress

Has this ever happened to you? It's the night before the big test and you're waiting to fall asleeeeeeeeep.

ZZZZzzzzzzzzzzzzz

Suddenly you hear: "Get up! You're late for school!" You run out the door just in time to see the bus driving away. Now you have to walk, but you . . . can't . . . seem . . . to . . . move. It's like you're wearing cement boots.

You finally make it to class, but the test has already started. You realize you forgot your pencil. You have a funny feeling you forgot something else, too. As you walk in, everyone laughs. You look down. **YIKES!** You forgot . . . your clothes.

Bad dreams like this are a sign of **TEST STRESS.**

What's Test Stress? It's when you're so worried about a test you can't think straight. Test Stress makes it hard to concentrate or pay attention. You may feel like you're wound up as tight as a ball of rubber bands.

This can lead to **TOTAL TERROR** on test day. By the time the test is passed out, you may be ready to pass out, too!

Test Stress makes you feel (choose the best answer):

confused

scared

nervous

helpless

anxious

sick

angry

doubtful

stupid

panicky

No matter which answer you picked, you're right! Test Stress can affect different people in different ways.

Five Signs of Test Stress

1. You freeze up during the test.

This is your brain.

This is your brain
on test day.

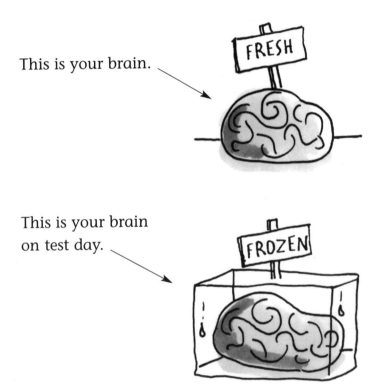

2. Your mind goes completely blank. It's like all the facts you once knew have floated out of your head and into someone else's.

3. You start wishing for a disaster.

4. You're so nervous that you don't even realize you're holding your breath. (If you start to turn blue, you need air—and fast!)

5. You feel like you're on the world's largest roller coaster—and the safety bar just broke.

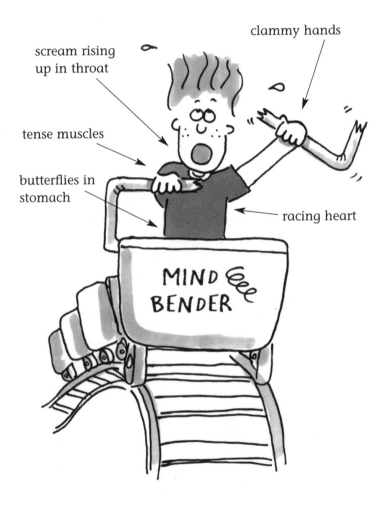

clammy hands

scream rising up in throat

tense muscles

butterflies in stomach

racing heart

MIND BENDER

If you're wondering why your mind and body react in these ways, here's the answer: People are naturally wired to respond to fear with what experts call the "fight-or-flight" response. This means your body wants to fight off or run away from something that's scary. This response may come in handy when you're faced with, say, a huge fire-breathing dragon—but not when you're about to take a math test!

Because you're stressed out, your mind races with thoughts like **"RUN FOR IT!"** and your body wants to obey. But you can't run from tests. You can't hide from them either. If you run and hide, a low grade will follow.

Besides, tests can be *verrrry* tricky. Sometimes they appear when you least expect them—as **POP QUIZZES!**

What happens when you have Test Stress and don't know how to handle it? You may begin to dislike your test. You may hate it with every bone in your body.

But if you spend all your time hating your test—

—you won't have time to take it!

Who Gets Test Stress?

The answer: *Anybody.* People of all ages (even adults) may get scared about tests.

Some people think the kids who get high grades just adore taking tests and don't *ever* have to deal with Test Stress.

After all, they're so smart they never have to worry about their grades, right?

WRONG!

In fact, many of the brightest students have *terrible* Test Stress. Why? Because they pressure themselves to be the best. For some, a low grade seems like the end of the world.

Kids who aren't doing well in school can get Test Stress, too. Each time they do poorly on a test, they feel dumb or frustrated. They may start to believe there's no chance they'll ever succeed. Some even stop studying or lose their desire to learn.

Tip: If you have trouble on tests and don't know what to do, if you can't seem to keep up in class, if you have school problems you don't know how to handle—talk to someone. Tell your teacher, your principal, or your mom or dad what you're going though. *Help is out there.*

Here's something very important to know: Experts believe Test Stress affects *how students do* on tests. Kids who are anxious about tests tend to score lower on them.

What can you do if this sounds like you? You can learn to tame test terror. Start by using the Anti-Test Stress Tip below.

Bang head here

WARNING: This is a joke! Do not try this at home (or anywhere else), unless you like to give yourself a headache!

How to Handle It

The first step in handling Test Stress is knowing when it happens. As soon as you start to feel jumpy, sick, or upset, tell yourself that **YOU** are bigger than your stress. Push stressful thoughts like "I'm going to fail" or "I'm so dumb" out of your mind. Tell yourself "I can do it!" Having a positive attitude helps.

Close your eyes and calm down. Take a long, slow, deep breath through your nose, slowly counting to five. Then breathe out through your nose, slowly counting backwards from five. Repeat this a few times and go back to your test. Breathing brings oxygen to your brain, which helps you think better.

One last thing: Tell yourself it's *only* a test. No one ever died from taking a test!

Test Your "Study Smarts"

Put this book down for a minute and get your backpack. Now look inside.

Is there:

- crumpled homework?
- a bunch of class notes with no date on them?
- a lot of *personal* notes from your friends?

- last week's assignment sheet you meant to finish?
- a moldy old sandwich?
- that library book you thought you lost?

- not a textbook in sight?

Uh-oh . . . it's time to improve your study habits!

To do well in school, you have to hit the books.

No! Hit the books doesn't mean *hit* the books! Hit the books means **STUDY.**

To do well on tests, you have to bring your textbooks home and **OPEN** them. If you play ten video games, hang out, clean your room, stare into space, go to the mall, and annoy your brother or sister for an hour before ever cracking a book, you're procrastinating. This means you're putting off what you shouldn't put off.

To study smart, get organized. Buy some color-coded folders for each subject (red for social studies, for example). Put all your loose notes, classwork, and homework in these folders so you have everything you need at your fingertips. Next, get a calendar to mark the days and times you plan to study.

Do you have a special *place* to study? Use a desk or table, and keep extra paper, pencils, pens, and a clock nearby. Be sure your study spot is well lighted (the light from the TV doesn't count).

If you have trouble getting motivated, find a **STUDY BUDDY.** Is there a friend or classmate (even a group of students) who might be able to help you?

You don't just get ready for a test the night before—you do it every single time you go to class. So take notes, listen, participate, and ask questions. After class, *review* your notes. After school, *review* what you learned that day. At least a week before your test, *review* your notes, homework, and textbook. Right before the test, *review* it all again.

This is a great way to **TRAIN YOUR BRAIN!**

You can use your finished tests as study tools. When you get a test back, don't just peek at your grade—check over each answer to see what you got right or wrong. Be sure to ask for the correct answers so you can learn from them.

BONUS: Teachers *have* been known to make mistakes. If you look over your test carefully, you may find a right answer that was accidentally marked wrong!

If you did well on your test, celebrate! Bring it home to show your family and display it on your bulletin board or refrigerator.

If you didn't do so well, don't waste energy feeling terrible. Instead, talk to your teacher and make a plan. What steps can you take to do better next time?

Want to know the greatest thing about tests? Once they're over, you feel terrific! Plus, when you do well on one, people are proud of you. Your teacher or friends at school might say "Good job!"

Best of all, you feel proud of *yourself.*

About the Authors

In addition to writing and illustrating, **Trevor Romain** regularly visits schools to speak to children. Trevor spends his free time with kids who have cancer at the Brackenridge Hospital in Austin, Texas.

Elizabeth Verdick has been a children's book editor for eight years and is the co-author of *Making Every Day Count: Daily Readings for Young People on Solving Problems, Setting Goals, & Feeling Good About Yourself* (Free Spirit Publishing, 1998). Elizabeth lives with her husband, two-year-old daughter, two cats, and a bunny in St. Paul, Minnesota.

Other Great Books from Free Spirit

How To Do Homework Without Throwing Up
by Trevor Romain

Hilarious cartoons and witty insights teach
important truths about homework and positive,
practical strategies for getting it done.
For ages 8–13.

$8.95; 72 pp.; softcover; illus.; 5⅛" x 7"

Bullies Are a Pain in the Brain
by Trevor Romain

Every child needs to know how to cope with
bullies. This book blends humor with practical
suggestions to help kids become "Bully-Proof."
For ages 8–13.

$9.95; 112 pp.; softcover; illus; 5⅛" x 7"

Cliques, Phonies, & Other Baloney
by Trevor Romain

Written for every kid who has ever felt
excluded or trapped by a clique, this book
blends humor with practical advice as it
tackles a serious subject. For ages 8–13.

$9.95; 136 pp.; softcover; illus.; 5⅛" x 7"

To place an order or to request a free catalog of materials,
please write, call, email, or visit our Web site:

Free Spirit Publishing Inc.
400 First Avenue North • Suite 616• Minneapolis, MN 55401-1724
call toll-free 800.735.7323 • or locally 612.338.2068 • fax 612.337.5050
help4kids@freespirit.com • www.freespirit.com

Visit us
on the Web!

www.freespirit.com

Our Web site gives you a fast and easy way to learn more about us, explore our catalog, order our books, meet our authors, and much more.

Just point and click!

new! Get the first look at our books, catch the latest news from Free Spirit, and check out our site's newest features.

contact Do you have a question for us or for one of our authors? Send us an email. Whenever possible, you'll receive a response within 48 hours.

order! Order in confidence! Our secure server uses the most sophisticated online ordering technology available. And ordering online is just one of the ways to purchase our books: you can also order by phone, fax, or regular mail. No matter which method you choose, excellent service is our goal.

1.800.735.7323 • fax 612.337.5050 • help4kids@freespirit.com